Amy -
   Just some
great reflections to
   read.
            Susan S

P. S. God, Can You Fly?

2

P. S. God, Can You Fly?

Heartfelt and Hope-Filled Prayers of Children

R. Wayne Willis

Westminster John Knox Press
LOUISVILLE • LONDON

© 2002 R. Wayne Willis

Bible quotations are the author's own translation.

Book design by Sharon Adams
Cover design by Teri Vinson
Illustrations by Serena Monique Dobson

First edition
Published by Westminster John Knox Press
Louisville, Kentucky

PRINTED IN THE UNITED STATES OF AMERICA

02 03 04 05 06 07 08 09 10 11 — 10 9 8 7 6 5 4 3 2 1

Library of Congress Cataloging-in-Publication Data

Willis, R. Wayne.
    P.S. God, can you fly? : heartfelt and hope-filled prayers of children / R. Wayne Willis. — 1st ed.
        p. cm.
    ISBN 0-664-22568-3 (pbk. : alk. paper)
    1. Children—Prayer-books and devotions—English. I. Title.

BV265 .W47 2001
242'.82—dc21
                                        2001040510

To the wee ones at Kosair Children's Hospital who, through no fault of their own, never got to ride rides and eat cotton candy, I dedicate this book.

Contents

Introduction

If you want to study the history of human flight, an ideal place to start is the National Air and Space Museum in Washington, D.C. To understand the life and times of Elvis Presley, the place to be is Graceland in Memphis, Tennessee. If you want to be awestruck by the beauty of nature, standing on the rim of the Grand Canyon at sunrise or sunset should help get you there. And if you want to plumb the depths of the human experience—explore the ultimate issues of life, its heights and depths—you should go to the chapels of Norton Hospital and Kosair Children's Hospital in Louisville, Kentucky.

For the past twenty-five years, visitors to these chapels have left behind traces of their spiritual struggles. They have inscribed thousands of three-by-five-inch cards with their doubts and dreams, fears and failures, sins and celebrations.

As the chaplain of these two hospitals for the past

quarter century, I have begun each day perusing and pondering the "straight from the heart" utterances left on the cards. I doubt that there exists anywhere on planet Earth a more intimate peek into the heart and soul—the DNA—of hurting people than we hold in this collection.

Children authored many of the cards. Picture a child, age five, accompanied by a parent or grandparent or sibling, or a solitary ten-year-old or fifteen-year-old, entering the chapel. The child knows the rules at school, at home, and in church. But in a hospital chapel, what's a child to do?

We have a record of what many children did. They transferred their soul's sincere desire (the traditional definition of prayer) onto paper. Then they left the prayer on the altar, inviting kindred strugglers who enter the chapel after them to share in their sentiments.

What makes their prayers unique? The prayers are remarkably *uninhibited.* Unbound by conventional notions of how prayers should be structured and worded, these children freely pray what they mean and mean what they pray. The result: prayer unflowery, unedited, unrefined, unvarnished—the kind of prayer not to be heard in a formal Sunday morning church service! Most of the prayers are starkly *urgent*. Children composed them, not in a classroom, not to satisfy a Sunday school teacher, but in the fiery furnace of a critical care hospital, where stakes—the life and health of a loved one—couldn't be higher.

What could children possibly teach grown-ups about prayer? Or about anything? After all, they're just little, inexperienced kids. What could they know that adults don't know? According to insightful adults over the ages—much!

Jesus: "*Unless you become like a little child, none of you will enter the kingdom of heaven.*" (Luke 18:17)

William Wordsworth: "*The Child is father of the Man.*"

Thomas Hood: "*I'm farther off from Heaven than when I was a boy.*"

Albert Einstein: "*Pay close attention to the curiosity of a child; this is where the search for knowledge is freshest and most valuable.*"

G. K. Chesterton: "*My first and last philosophy, that which I believe in with unbroken certainty, I learnt in the nursery.*"

Pablo Picasso: "*Every child is an artist. The problem is how to remain an artist once one grows up.*"

Robert Fulghum: "*Everything I need to know I learned in kindergarten.*"

In *Thus Spake Zarathustra*, Nietzsche divided adult development into three stages. The first is represented by the camel: "Load me down; I can take it." The lion symbolizes the second stage: "Get off my back; I'm tired of trying to meet everyone else's expectations." Stage three, for those who reach it, is the stage of the child, who embraces all of life freely and joyfully, as pure wonderment, pure gift.

There's something primal and pristine and pure, something relatively uncontaminated issuing from the hearts and minds of little ones, something near the deep-down mysteries and meanings of life. Children's theological credentials derive, according to Jesus, from their special proximity and access to the heart of God: "*Never discount one of these little ones; I tell you, they have their guardian angels in heaven who look continually on the face of the heavenly Father*" (Matt. 18:10).

I have selected thirty children's prayers for their simple profundity. My accompanying commentary suggests that the prayers shed light on life's ultimate issues—on prayer, on God, on meaning, virtue, and truth.

I trust you will find that the prayers illustrate Isaiah's ancient wisdom: *"And a little child shall lead them"* (Isa. 11:6).

R. Wayne Willis
Louisville, Kentucky

†♥†

Thank you
Lord for not
letting it be
any worst.
I love you.

†♥†

Reality Check

"Thank you Lord for not letting it be any worst. I love you."

There are few things like a visit to the hospital for a reality check, for putting life in perspective.

One day I entered the burn unit of our children's hospital and my eyes immediately fixed on a new patient. He was seated in his room's doorway in a wheelchair, bound in gauze from his waist up, with holes in the facial wrap for eyes, nose, mouth, and ears. I couldn't tell whether the child was a boy or a girl until he told me his name. His name was Paul. He was five years old. Paul told me he had been badly burned in a fire at his house the day before. I noticed on his nightstand a beautiful medal and asked him what it was. He told me how a uniformed policeman had entered the unit earlier that day to visit someone else. When his eyes and Paul's eyes met, Paul attempted a wave with his rigid arm. The wave attempt stopped the policeman in his tracks. He turned and left the unit. He returned a short time later with a Medal of Honor in his hand, a medal he had been awarded two weeks earlier. He walked into Paul's room, draped the medal around Paul's neck, and told him, "You deserve this more than I do. You're a hero. This is for you." Then he turned and walked away.

What happened inside the policeman happens inside many of us who work with sick people. We find it hard, seeing the world from inside a hospital, to get overwrought at a fender bender, a correction in the stock market, or a rained-out golf game. Glimpses of a sixteen-year-old girl bald from chemotherapy or a ten-year-old boy with severe cerebral palsy or a five-year-old burned child help us, as it did the policeman, keep a sense of proportion and balance to life. Exposure to suffering helps us check our urge to complain about what we lack and feel more gratitude for what we have. It compels us to "cleave ever," as Tennyson said, "to the sunnier side of doubt."

Sensitized by the sufferers of the world, we side with Emerson: "Give me health and a day, and I will make the pomp of emperors ridiculous." We find whiners—those who say the porridge is too hot or too cold, the chair too hard or too soft—hard to abide. We have to practice patience with our friends and neighbors who haven't had the benefit of seeing what we have seen and, thus, knowing what we know about the tenuous nature of health and life.

Life puts a question to each of us daily: On balance, do we tilt toward the *sunnier* or the *cloudier* side of doubt? Do we tend to see a day mixed with clouds as partly *cloudy* or partly *sunny*? Do we see 50 percent of married people *getting divorced*, or 50 percent of married people *staying married*? Do we tend to rejoice because of the roses on the thornbush or complain about the thorns on the rosebush? Does the most beautiful day in May evoke a "Wow!" or a dread of the miserably hot summer days fast approaching? Does the perfect autumn day evoke a "Wow!" or a dread of leaf-raking and heating bills and inclement weather?

A visit to the hospital could tip the balance.

Lord, please help a little
boy who fell off a house.
And please help a lady
who's daughter is not only
blind but is very sick.
And also help my grandpa
to get better and to
breathe better.

Cross Over the Bridge

*"Lord, please help a little boy who fell off a house.
And please help a lady who's daughter is not only
blind but is very sick. And also help my grandpa to
get better and to breathe better."*

James Baldwin, who grew up in Harlem during the
Depression, was born with "frog eyes." His stepfather
regularly said to him, "You are the ugliest boy I have ever
seen." Baldwin went on to write the highly acclaimed
Nobody Knows My Name and *Go Tell It on the Mountain*. James Baldwin, a prince of a writer who began life
as a frog, reflecting on his pained childhood wrote, "At
some point you have to realize that your suffering does
not isolate you; your suffering is your bridge."

Suffering was the bridge for Gautama. His parents reared him in a palace and tried to spare him any exposure to the harsh side of life. Even when his chari- oteer took him on outings, servants went before them and decorated the way and removed ugly or unpleas- ant sights that might upset the sheltered prince. But on one trip Gautama accidentally saw a wrinkled old man with white hair, bent over and walking with a stick— and he learned about aging. On another outing he saw an emaciated, pale, diseased man—and he learned about illness. On another he saw dirty, sweaty slaves working, and oxen with heavy yokes that rubbed the hide from their shoulders—and he learned about involuntary servitude. On yet another he came across a funeral procession and saw the corpse—and he learned about death. Moved by those exposures to the real world, Gautama abandoned the ivory palace and dedicated the rest of his life to developing a philoso- phy—building a bridge—to sufferers. Gautama Bud- dha set as the first of Buddhism's four noble truths, the one from which the others derive: "Life is suffering."

Suffering is a bridge for people thrown together in a hospital's waiting room. In that room, suffering tran- scends all the differences that keep people outside the hospital apart. Suffering becomes the great equalizer, bridging the gap between believers and unbelievers, haves and have-nots, Jews and Gentiles, Buddhists and Baptists, youngsters and oldsters.

One little girl who came to the hospital to visit her grandfather felt moved to write a prayer before she left. She prayed, not just for her grandfather, but first for two strangers: "a little boy who fell off a house" and "a lady who's daughter is not only blind but very sick." Exposure to suffering pierced her tender heart and enlarged her soul.

Each of us is building either a bridge or a pier. A pier stands alone, goes nowhere, connects to nothing. Suffering builds a bridge, a bridge that tenderizes and humanizes those who cross over it.

†♥†

Please be with grandma even though she's a Jova Witness (cause we still love her). She is still one of your children.

†♥†

Big Blue Marble

"Please be with grandma even though she's a Jova Witness (cause we still love her). She is still one of your children."

Mariners, back at the dawn of civilization, drew crude maps of coastlines for navigational purposes. Geographers converted those drawings into charts. Those charts put empires, territories, and countries in their proper places. It was late in the nineteenth century before hot-air balloons were able to rise thousands of feet above the ground and photograph a small fraction of planet Earth. Airplanes and rockets eventually flew high enough to make pictures of Earth that showed its curvature.

But it was the Apollo astronauts who viewed, for the first time, the whole earth. They reported from their 1968 Apollo 8 trip around the moon that "the earth's a big blue marble when you see it from up here." With their view from a distance came a new paradigm for us earthlings. From a distance, Earth has no nations, no state lines, no borders. The "big blue marble" paradigm helps us see all forms of nationalism as, at best, limited, and at worst, silly. Provincialism—applying our own province's standards and customs to the rest of the planet—exposes a contrived, limited, dated, pre-big-blue-marble point of view.

In religion, a similar tension always exists between the whole and its parts. There will always be some who are drawn to sectarian religion. Sectarianism thrives on exclusion, on self-righteously justifying one "province" of religious interpretation to the exclusion of all others. That spirit spawned centuries of holy wars and hatred, prejudice and persecution. And the god of sectarians always just happens to think and look like them. As the early Greek philosopher Xenophanes wrote, "The Ethiopians make their gods black and snub-nosed; the Thracians say theirs have blue eyes and red hair. . . . If oxen and horses or lions had hands and could produce works of art as men do, horses would paint the forms of gods like horses and oxen like oxen."

A few religious contrarians in every age rise above sectarianism to know the *mysterium tremendum et fascinans*, God too grand to be captured and contained in doctrinal and creedal cages. Contrarians identify with the humility of Mechthild of Magdeburg, the thirteenth-century poet who wrote, "Of the heavenly things God has shown me, I can speak but a little word, not more than a honeybee can carry away on its foot from an overflowing jar." Contrarians resonate with the spirit and perspective of Gandhi, who said, "I am Hindu. I am Christian. I am Muslim. I am Jew."

The child in the chapel prays for his grandmother, who happens to be a Jehovah's Witness. He has been taught that Jehovah's Witnesses are inferior, defective in some way—brainwashed or weird or duped or dangerous or something. The child is torn—despite the magnitude of her heresy, she is his grandma, and he loves her.

He sees his sick grandmother first, a religious label second. He illustrates Agatha Christie's truth: "If you stick too rigidly to your principles, you'll hardly see anyone." The grandson's instincts are good—magnanimous and charitable. He drew a big blue circle that took her in.

✝ ♥ ✝ ♥ ✝ ♥ ✝ ♥ ✝ ♥ ✝ ♥ ✝ ♥ ✝ ♥ ✝ ♥ ✝ ♥ ✝ ♥ ✝ ♥ ✝ ♥ ✝ ♥ ✝ ♥ ✝ ♥ ✝

Dear God,

Please help my
Father. Please
do not take him
yet. let him
talk to us
just one more time.

✝ ♥ ✝ ♥ ✝ ♥ ✝ ♥ ✝ ♥ ✝ ♥ ✝ ♥ ✝ ♥ ✝ ♥ ✝ ♥ ✝ ♥ ✝ ♥ ✝ ♥ ✝ ♥ ✝ ♥ ✝ ♥ ✝

The Blessing

"Dear God, Please help my father. Please do not take him yet. Let him talk to us just one more time."

"We live by affirmations," Victor Hugo wrote, "more than bread."

Children crave words of blessing from authority figures. The blessing sometimes becomes the gift that turns a life and lasts a lifetime.

Pablo Picasso was a failure as a schoolboy. He exasperated his teachers who tried to teach him reading, writing, and arithmetic. But his mother believed in his potential and one day said to him, "Pablo, if you decide to become a soldier when you grow up, you'll make general. If you decide to become a priest, you'll make Pope." That affirmation ultimately outweighed the opposing messages Pablo brought home from school. He tucked away in his heart the notion that he carried greatness within him.

Jesse Stuart left a remarkably undistinguished mark in school. However, in Mrs. Hamilton's history class one day he made a comment that moved Mrs. Hamilton to say before the whole class, "Why Jesse, you sound just like a future Patrick Henry." Mrs. Hamilton perhaps forgot by the next day that she ever made that statement. But Jesse never forgot. Decades later, having become one of America's most loved writers and Kentucky's poet laureate, Jesse Stuart affectionately remembered the day Mrs. Hamilton put in a good word for him.

David Brinkley's mother was forty-two years old when he was born. To still be having babies at that age was in that day and age considered scandalous to her and her women friends, and when David was born she cried uncontrollably for days. One day when little David wrote something and showed it to his mother for her approval, she threw the paper in his face and said,

"Why are you wasting your time on this foolishness?" Denied the blessing at home, David found it in Mrs. Smith's high school English class. One day she said to him, "David, I think you ought to be a journalist." About that vote of confidence, David Brinkley—world-class journalist—reflected in his autobiography, "A world turned for me."

Parents and grandparents hold the strategic high ground for conferring the blessing, for getting the message to the impressionable child: "You are great with divinity. You are good stuff. I believe in you. Go forth, spread your wings, and soar."

Christopher Morley once said that if we suddenly discovered we had only five minutes to live, every phone booth in the country would be filled with people blurting out, "I love you."

Why wait until the last five minutes?

Dear   God,
Thank you for
letting me
live and
keeping me
alive.
PS can you
fly?

I'll Fly Away

"Dear God, Thank you for letting me live and keeping me alive. PS can you fly?"

Peter Pan represents that childlike aspect of ourselves that doesn't want to grow up, and, for our own spiritual good, shouldn't. But unfortunately, the more sophisticated we get, the more likely we are to leave our playful, lovable, imaginative, joyful, childlike self behind.

There was a time in the history of the world, just as there was a time in our youth, when the universe teemed with mystery. Angels and demons, gnomes and trolls, ghosts and goblins, witches and werewolves populated the heavens and earth. That was a time when animals and rocks and bushes spoke, planetary alignments caused plagues, and people sprouted wings and flew. Wonder reigned.

Then the scientific revolution came along, and natural explanations solved many of the old puzzlements. Science scoured the world clean of spirits. Rationality exposed miracles as primitive superstition. Reason scrubbed the awe and wonder out of religion. The scientific method held forth the promise that, with time, it would rid the world of all its unknowns.

And yet, as we become more and more enlightened, there remains deep within us a craving, in the words of William Butler Yeats, to "clap hands and sing."

That side of us given to marvel and miracle, we now know from the study of soldiers who sustained brain injuries in World War II, is the brain's right hemisphere. The right side imagines and intuits, worships and wonders. While the right side sees the big picture, the left side works with logic and language. If we are to be whole, both halves of this magnificent two-cylinder machine need to be in play.

What does it mean to have a healthy right brain, to become, as Jesus said we should, "like a little child" (Matt. 18:1)? It means to keep alive within us the sense of awe and wonder and imagination and mystery that shone through our eyes when we were five years old.

Some call that capacity "beginner's mind." Suzuki Roshi wrote, "In the beginner's mind there are many possibilities; in the expert's mind there are few."

Some call it staying "green." Hildegard of Bingen wrote, "Let us keep greenness in our souls so that creation can still unfold in us no matter what the season. Keep the soul moist so growth can continue."

"Naïveté," Goethe wrote, "is the most important attribute of genius."

The query of God by the child in the chapel queries us grown-ups as well: "Can you fly?"

Dear Lord
I'm Sorry I
Stold the
Quarter

Tenderheart

"Dear Lord, I'm sorry I stold the quarter."

She didn't claim that the devil made her do it. She didn't blame listening to rap lyrics, attending a Marilyn Manson concert, reading gang graffiti, eating Twinkies, playing video games, or chatting on the Internet. Tenderheart, we could call her, simply placed on the chapel's altar a humble confession: "I'm sorry I stold the quarter."

Some people give guilt—a perfectly healthy emotion—a bad name. They are the guilt junkies who have cultivated a habit of coddling regrets and dwelling on failures. They beat themselves up over everything from problems their kids have in school to the kind of kids they were to their own parents way back when. Wallowing in the muck, obviously, is no way to get clean.

On the opposite end of the spectrum are those who, for whatever reason, never developed much of a capacity for guilt. They freely use and abuse others, feeling no pangs of conscience. Sometimes these guilt-free persons have to be locked up for the safety of the rest of us.

But healthy guilt is one of humankind's noblest emotions. According to psychiatrist Willard Gaylin, it is "the guardian of our goodness." Guilt leads us to say, "I'm sorry." Guilt moves us to make amends, to refrain from hurting others, to visit a relative in a nursing home, to drop a coin in the Salvation Army kettle, to call home, to treat the kids to a day in the park. Feeling guilt is one of the primary indicators that we are moral and human.

Instinct-driven snails and salmon feel no guilt. But we humans, between the stimulus and our response, have an opportune moment, a "pregnant pause" in which we choose what we will do. When our response turns out wrong or hurtful or both, we then have a second choice to make. Shall we deep-six it? Burying it is like leaving a splinter of wood in a finger. The tissue around it festers. Covering it up is like hiding the kitchen garbage in drawers and closets, under the bed and behind the door. It may be out of sight, but in time it will putrefy and foul the house. Stuffing it is about as effective as applying compresses or rouge to a boil. What guilt needs is not camouflage, but release. Nature begs us to express it, to let it go.

Tenderheart models for us how to keep failures from spoiling life. She takes the first giant step, which is to make honest confession, to "undress the soul at night," as George Herbert advised. Step two is to right the wrong as best we can—return the quarter. Step three is to voice with Charlie Brown one or two strong "Rats!," get off the guilt trip, and get on with life.

✝ ♥ ✝ ♥ ✝ ♥ ✝ ♥ ✝ ♥ ✝ ♥ ✝ ♥ ✝ ♥ ✝ ♥ ✝ ♥ ✝ ♥ ✝ ♥ ✝ ♥ ✝ ♥ ✝ ♥ ✝ ♥ ✝ ♥ ✝ ♥ ✝

Dear God
I was prying that you
could let him live 100%
Perfect like a normal child
he has never got to rid a ride
or eat cotton candy in his
life. So IF you can Pleas let
him live a long and happy life.

✝ ♥ ✝ ♥ ✝ ♥ ✝ ♥ ✝ ♥ ✝ ♥ ✝ ♥ ✝ ♥ ✝ ♥ ✝ ♥ ✝ ♥ ✝ ♥ ✝ ♥ ✝ ♥ ✝ ♥ ✝ ♥ ✝ ♥ ✝ ♥ ✝

Cotton Candy

"Dear God, I was prying that you could let him live 100% perfect like a normal child. He has never got to rid a ride or eat cotton candy in his life. So if you can pleas let him live a long and happy life."

In the name of all that's fair, shouldn't childhood be a time of innocence, play, and fun? Joan Walsh Anglund said as much in *Morning Is a Little Child:* "And the duty of children is *fun*."

For most of history, however, childhood has been anything but fun. For example, almost all child-rearing literature from antiquity into the twentieth century recommended beating children. One nineteenth-century German schoolmaster reported administering 911,527 strokes from a stick; 124,000 lashes with a whip; 136,715 slaps with his hand; and 1,115,800 boxes on the ear. Beethoven whipped his piano students with a knitting needle. John Milton's wife complained of hating to hear the cries of his nephews as he beat them. Children had no laws protecting them. They were totally at the mercy of the big people near them.

Classic fairy tales graphically portray the violence and cruelty of childhood. When Pinocchio veered from Geppetto's orders, his legs were burned off, or his nose grew longer, or he was hung from a fruit tree, or he was imprisoned for four months, or he was swallowed by a shark. In the story of Snow White, the queen ordered the hunter to kill Snow White and bring back her lungs and liver as proof. A wolf tried to devour Little Red Riding Hood. Hansel and Gretel's parents abandoned them in the woods to wild animals. Far from frivolous and carefree, childhood was dangerous and scary. Kids were lucky to survive it.

Have we progressed? In 1940, the top disciplinary problems in schools were talking out of turn, chewing gum, making noise, running in the halls, cutting in line, wearing improper clothing, and not putting paper in the wastebasket. In the 1990s, they were drug abuse, alcohol abuse, pregnancy, suicide, rape, robbery, and assault.

The world we have inherited, in philosopher Bertrand Russell's words, "is horrible, horrible, horrible." Babies are born with birth defects. Elementary school kids get cancer and die. Where's the justice, by anyone's standard, in that?

Albert Camus once told a gathering of Dominican monks, "Perhaps we cannot prevent this world from being a world in which children are tortured. But we can reduce the number of tortured children. And if you don't help us, who else in the world can?"

People of goodwill work to build a world in which more kids get a childhood. That means, among other things, a chance to "rid a ride or eat cotton candy."

†♥†

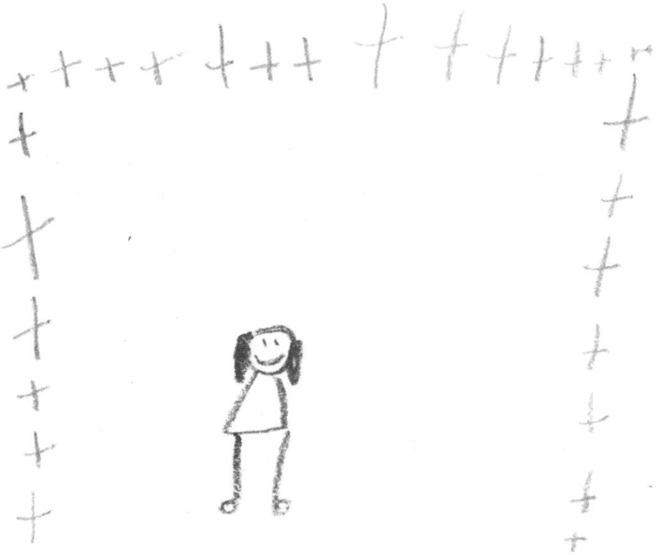

†♥†

Security Blanket

In a Peanuts cartoon, Charlie Brown explains to Peppermint Patty what security is: "Security is sleeping in the back seat of the car. When you're a little kid, and you've been somewhere with your mom and dad, and it's night, and you're riding home in the car, you can sleep in the back seat. You don't have to worry about anything. Your mom and dad are in the front seat, and they do all the worrying. They take care of everything."

Charles Schultz's genius was his ability to translate life's most basic, universal experiences into simple cartoon form. We can identify, for example, with Linus and his blue flannel blanket that he dragged everywhere because we intuitively know what that blanket represents. It stands for our lifelong desire to trust life, to feel relatively safe in an unsafe world, to believe that out of this universe we cannot fall. Charlie Brown explains to Peppermint Patty how grown-ups tend to lose that sense of basic trust they knew as a child: "It doesn't last! Suddenly, you're grown up and it can never be that way again. Suddenly, it's over, and you'll never get to sleep in the back seat again! Never!"

Charles Dickens's Miss Havisham in *Great Expectations* stands as literature's most unforgettable example of lost trust. The only man Miss Havisham ever loved sent her a letter on their wedding day that called off the wedding. The letter came at 8:40 A.M., while she was putting on her wedding dress. She stopped all the clocks in the house at that time, sealed up every window, and never took off her wedding dress. The wedding cake hardened and collected cobwebs and dust. She drew all the drapes so that sunshine would never enter the house again. A flickering candle was the only light in her gloomy room. The wedding gown, over the years, yellowed on her shrunken body. She never trusted again. And no man ever let her down again.

The young artist who drew the armless person surrounded by crosses knew trust. Perhaps she could not spell trust. She probably could not define trust or intelligently discuss religious categories like faith and hope. Her feeling of helplessness or lack of control is apparent in the figure she drew that had no arms. Despite her powerlessness, she felt surrounded and protected— encircled—by God's love, what religious people call "the everlasting arms," which she signified with plusses or crosses. That sense of basic trust emboldened her to finish off the portrait with a smiley face. She illustrates what Susan Howatch asserted in *Ultimate Prizes:* "Sometimes mere words are no good. In the presence of suffering, only symbols have meaning."

How important it is for us adults to reestablish contact with the child down deep inside us who once knew trust, the child who can go to sleep in the back seat believing that someone trustworthy is at the wheel.

✝♥✝♥✝♥✝♥✝♥✝♥✝♥✝♥✝♥✝♥✝♥✝♥✝♥✝♥✝♥✝♥✝

Please pray for my
sister who has asthma
She's 7 + my brother
who's 2 he has a
hole in his heart
and for me I'm 13
who has juvinile
reumatoid arthritis,

✝♥✝♥✝♥✝♥✝♥✝♥✝♥✝♥✝♥✝♥✝♥✝♥✝♥✝♥✝♥✝♥✝

Egomaniac

*"Please pray for my sister who has asthma she's 7 &
my brother who's 2 he has a hole in his heart and
for me I'm 13 who has juvinile reumatoid arthritis."*

I want to tell you about the most unforgettable house-
guest we ever had.

In a word, he was an egomaniac. He expected us to
do everything for him, and he did nothing—literally
nothing—for himself. All he wanted was what he
wanted when he wanted it. He was capable of not one
shred of flexibility. He demanded that we drop everything, whatever his need, and give our undivided attention to satisfying him.

We felt most imposed on at mealtime. He would not eat when or what we ate. Whenever he got hungry—morning, noon, or night—he vigorously protested. And impatient! When we were a little slow getting the food out, he fussed at us. Did he ever offer to help prepare the meal? Did he once lift a finger to clean up afterwards? Not once. We did all the bending, all the giving. It was a totally lopsided arrangement.

And dirty! He stank much of the time. Personal hygiene was a foreign language to him. He never bathed himself, never washed his clothes or changed the sheets. It bothered him not one whit. Cleanliness wasn't next to godliness; it simply wasn't.

And noisy! Sometimes in the wee small hours of the morning he would decide it was time to get up and visit. Many days we went off to work sleep-deprived from a 2 A.M. visit.

Our guest was your total freeloader. He never contributed one dime to help out with expenses. He stayed and stayed, mooched and mooched, taking it for granted that we existed only to serve him.

The identity of our guest? He was our infant son. Today, he has grown out of self-absorption and become a mature adult, able to love neighbor as well as self, able to practice altruism. He's very fortunate. Many people never make the transition. They spend their lifetime stuck in infantile egocentrism.

The thirteen-year-old who penned this prayer has, at a tender age, successfully migrated from a me-me-me solar system, bounded on the west by an "m" and the east by an "e." She prays first for her sister, then for her brother, and last for herself.

It is children like her who warm up this cold planet and make it—for all of us—a more hospitable place to be.

† ♥ † ♥ † ♥ † ♥ † ♥ † ♥ † ♥ † ♥ † ♥ † ♥ † ♥ † ♥ † ♥ † ♥ † ♥ † ♥ † ♥ † ♥ † ♥ †

my mom is Die why
Do God Love me
why! I Love my mother very
very much. I pray for her.
I call God for help But she
Die

† ♥ † ♥ † ♥ † ♥ † ♥ † ♥ † ♥ † ♥ † ♥ † ♥ † ♥ † ♥ † ♥ † ♥ † ♥ † ♥ † ♥ † ♥ † ♥ †

Living the Questions

"My mom is die. Why. Do God love me. Why! I love my mother very very much. I pray for her. I call God for help but she die."

Once Mother Teresa comforted a very sick little girl with these words: "You should be happy that God sends you suffering. Sufferings are proof that God loves you very much. Your sufferings are kisses from Jesus." The little girl replied, "Mother, please ask Jesus to stop kissing me so much."

A grief-stricken mother in our hospital emergency room was explaining to her five-year-old son why his infant sister had died. "God just needed another little angel," the mother explained. Her son, lower lip extended, blubbered back, "You would think God has enough little angels by now."

All our fanciest theologies, all our most cleverly devised explanations fall about three giant steps short of solving life's greatest riddle—why good people, especially innocent children, suffer.

The hiddenness of God, what the theologians call *deus absconditus*, has perplexed and confounded the great saints of the ages. St. John of the Cross once prayed, "I sometimes think you are mocking me by hiding yourself from me." Johann Starck, eighteenth-century pietist, prayed, "My God, you have plunged me into such sorrow and anguish that my eyes are swollen with tears, and even the beat of my heart is hard and irregular. Was I not happy once?" The Psalmist cried out, "Why are you so far from helping me, from the words of my groaning? O my God, I cry by day, but you do not answer; and by night, but find no rest" (Psalm 22:1–2). Even the founder of Christianity felt the absence, the abandonment of God. He wailed from the cross, "My God, my God, why have you forsaken me?" (Matt. 27:46).

There may be no perfectly satisfying answer to

"Why?" But there is a solution. The solution lies not in words and sermons, doctrines and explanations. The solution lies in faithful friendships—people who hear us out, who hang in there with us through thick and thin. They are those individuals who sit with us in the rubble of our lives, say "I don't know" when they don't know, accept our woundedness without preaching to us, are there for us after others—worn out by our anguish—have withdrawn. Those people are the solution, not because they have the answers, but because they help us live with and through the questions.

Ranier Maria Rilke said it best: "Be patient toward all that is unsolved in your heart, and try to love the questions themselves like locked rooms and like books that are written in a foreign tongue. Live everything. Live the questions now. Perhaps you will then gradually, without noticing it, live some distant day into the answer."

† ♥ † ♥ † ♥ † ♥ † ♥ † ♥ † ♥ † ♥ † ♥ † ♥ † ♥ † ♥ † ♥ † ♥ † ♥ † ♥ †

I know that I have sinned. But could you please forgive me for all my sins, and help me pass through the sixth grade?

† ♥ † ♥ † ♥ † ♥ † ♥ † ♥ † ♥ † ♥ † ♥ † ♥ † ♥ † ♥ † ♥ † ♥ † ♥ † ♥ †

The Big Holy

"I know that I have sinned. But could you please forgive me for all my sins, and help me pass through the sixth grade?"

Why do children so naturally pray about sacred and secular things in the same breath? Because no adult has yet taught them to make that artificial, dichotomous distinction.

Luther Standing Bear, Sioux chief, said of his people, "The Indian loved to worship. From birth to death he revered his surroundings. He considered himself born in the luxurious lap of Mother Earth. No place to him was humble. There was nothing between him and The Big Holy."

Nothing stands between children and The Big Holy. Unlike adults, children don't divide the world into secular things and sacred things, common things and holy things. Prayer for forgiveness of sins and prayer to pass through the sixth grade are equally appropriate prayers. Both are from the same piece of cloth. The fabric is life. Both are part of The Big Holy.

Another child wrote a prayer in the chapel ". . . for mom to get to feeling better, and for me to have the courage to ask Connie out to our banquet. And Lord, help her to say yes, because I really like her. Amen." Prayer for a date with Connie merits an amen, just as much as prayer for her mom's health. Connie's company and her mom's health both fall within The Big Holy.

Unlike children, many adults split reality into two parts. They turn the *universe* into a *duoverse*. Sunday is for sowing to the sacred, the other six days of the week for sowing to the secular. Some adults cleave personal life from professional life. They come off one way at work, but when they cross the threshold of home, watch out—their family sees someone else. To these people, one territory is part of The Big Holy; the other is not.

Some people split the human being into two distinct parts. There's the body, tended by physicians, and there's the spirit, tended by clergy. Splitters deny that helplessness and hopelessness cause disease and death, that faith and hope and love heal. They discount the proverb, "A merry heart does good like a medicine, but a sad spirit dries up the bones" (Prov. 17:22).

Why does the Native American shed a tear over the pollution of rivers and streams? Why are so many people turned off to sermons and doctrines that play well in a house of worship but are irrelevant to school and work?

Children believe that all of life is a part of The Big Holy. Their theological message to us adults might be, to use the title of J. B. Phillips's book, "Your God is too small."

✝♥✝

God please heal
my sore throat
and tummy
acke.

Amen.

✝♥✝

K. I. S. S.

"God please heal my sore throat and tummy acke. Amen."

The more cluttered and complicated life gets, the more we crave a saner, simpler way.

If there were a Simplicity Hall of Fame, Henry David Thoreau would surely be in it. He lived alone in a cabin in the woods for a couple of years. It was his observation that the masses of people "live lives of quiet desperation" that drove him there. From the woods by Walden Pond comes this insight: "Life is frittered away by detail. Simplify. Simplify."

Abraham Lincoln would make the Simplicity Hall of

Fame with his Gettysburg address. The greatest speech in American history is famous not just because of what Lincoln said, but because he said it in two minutes. Edward Everett, the greatest orator of the day, preceded Lincoln with a speech that lasted two hours. No one remembers what he said.

Albert Einstein's outfit would be displayed in the Simplicity Hall of Fame. He wore the same old sweater and baggy pants, day after day, year after year. He said it was a good habit because it cut down on daily decision making. Not having to decide which clothes to wear freed him up to focus on more important matters.

Religion sometimes gets too complicated for ordinary mortals. We forget that Moses came down the mountain with ten, not ten thousand, commandments. To those who had made religion too complicated, who were majoring in minors, the prophet Micah said, "What does the Lord require of you but to do justice, practice kindness, and walk humbly with God?" (Micah 6:8). To those who had made religion too complicated, who were majoring in minors, Jesus said, "All God's requirements can be summed up in one sentence—love God and love your neighbor as yourself" (Matt. 22:40).

Children who leave written prayers in the hospital chapel help us see that prayer in its purest form is not a fancy, frilly, flowery performance. Prayer is simply an expression of the soul's sincere desire. No effort to impress, flatter, or manipulate God. No need to explain or belabor the details. Just: "God please heal my sore throat and tummy acke. Amen."

The patron saint of children's prayers could be Dr. Seuss's Horace the Elephant: "He meant what he said and he said what he meant. An elephant's faithful one hundred percent."

The popular acrostic K.I.S.S. can remind us grown-ups of the truth about prayer—and about life—that the children already know: "Keep it simple, stupid!"

† ♥ † ♥ † ♥ † ♥ † ♥ † ♥ † ♥ † ♥ † ♥ † ♥ † ♥ † ♥ † ♥ † ♥ † ♥ † ♥ † ♥ †

I love him. I wish he could come home with us this very day.

† ♥ † ♥ † ♥ † ♥ † ♥ † ♥ † ♥ † ♥ † ♥ † ♥ † ♥ † ♥ † ♥ † ♥ † ♥ † ♥ † ♥ †

Coming Home

"I love him. I wish he could come home with us this very day."

Few words in the English language pack so much emotion.

When E.T., near the end of Stephen Spielberg's *E.T., The Extraterrestrial*, pointed his crooked, bony finger toward the heavens, one mournful syllable passed his alien lips: "Home!"

After following the yellow brick road and sampling all the sights and thrills of utopian Oz, Dorothy spoke the sentence that has become a cliché in our day: "There's no place like home." The scarecrow wanted brains. The lion wanted courage. The tin man wanted a heart. Despite the tornadoes and boring landscape of Kansas, despite the fact that bankers held the mortgage on Uncle Henry and Auntie Em's farm, Dorothy just wanted to go home.

That four-letter word is likely the last word on the lips of the soldier dying on the desert sand or in a rice paddy halfway around the world. It may be the one syllable throbbing in the frontal lobe of the college student as she completes her last final and hits the road, visions of home-cooked food and smiling faces and warm embraces and sounds of "Good to see you!" dancing in her head.

Sadly, for some of us, "home" is an unpleasant association. It peels back a scab of painful memories—of abuse or conflict or rejection. Some of us unfortunately remember home not as a shelter from the storms of life that we ran *to*, but a place of hurt we couldn't wait to get away *from*.

But home is really not that much about geography. Home is not a house. Nor is it necessarily our family of origin. Home is the people who, when we're with them, delight in having us there.

All the hospital employees knew or at least knew of

the baby boy nicknamed "Bear." He began life with a lethal condition. No one but his family believed he would survive. They were always there for him, month in and month out, cheering him on, delighting in every small victory, hoping against hope that if they could "buy some more time" a cure would be found. They couldn't take Bear home, so they brought home to Bear. The story has a happy ending. A wonderful physician–wonderful family combination saved the doomed baby. Today he is a healthy, thriving teenager.

Home is the people who know us and accept us as we are—warts and all. Home is, instead of a location, the people who believe in us and take us in, the people who, when we're with them, delight in having us there.

✝♥✝♥✝♥✝♥✝♥✝♥✝♥✝♥✝♥✝♥✝♥✝♥✝♥✝♥✝♥✝♥✝♥✝♥✝♥✝

Pray that me &
Don hook up!

Thank
You!

✝♥✝♥✝♥✝♥✝♥✝♥✝♥✝♥✝♥✝♥✝♥✝♥✝♥✝♥✝♥✝♥✝♥✝♥✝♥✝

Discovering Fire

"Pray that me & Don hook up! Thank you!"

What's it all about? When all is said and done, it's only about "hooking up."

In the movie *Don Juan DeMarco,* a wise psychiatrist, played by Marlon Brando, explains the facts of life to Don Juan: "There are only four questions in life. What is sacred? What is spirit made of? What is worth dying for? What is worth living for? The answer to all four is the same—love, only love."

Love seizes us by surprise from time to time, driving us to take enormous risks to overcome our halfness and become whole. It is that force that persistently prods and pulls at us to break out of the prison of our alone-ness and "hook up"—fully relate—to another. That is the irresistible force that drove Romeo and Juliet into each other's arms, uniting the Montague and Capulet families and ultimately the entire city of Verona. Of life's ultimate force Paul wrote in his great ode to love, "It still stands when all else has fallen . . . Make love your aim."

A thirteen-year-old boy named Tad was unconscious for weeks in our hospital following brain surgery. Learn-ing that the two senses unconscious patients lose last are touch and hearing, Tad's parents, who never left his side, wrote love messages on construction paper and taped them over the head of his bed. The messages instructed everyone who entered the room: "I like to be called Tad." "When you talk to me, rub my hands and arms." "Say positive things to me like, 'You're getting stronger, Tad.'" Even unconsciousness, Tad's parents believed and hospital staff believe, is subject to the power of love.

How important in life is "hooking up"?

More important than anything, according to eighteenth-century philosopher David Hume: "Let all the powers and elements of nature conspire to serve and obey one man; let the sun rise and set at his command; the sea and rivers roll as he pleases; the earth furnish spontaneously whatever may be useful or agreeable to him. He will still be miserable till you give him one person at least with whom he may share his happiness, and whose esteem and friendship he may enjoy."

More important than anything, according to twentieth-century French Jesuit and philosopher Teilhard de Chardin: "Someday, after we have mastered the winds, the waves, the tides and gravity, we shall harness the energies of love. Then, for the second time in the history of the world, we will have discovered fire."

Everything else is just posturing. Scaffolding. Background music. Prologue.

It's all about "hooking up." So make love your aim. It alone stands when all else falls.

† ♥ † ♥ † ♥ † ♥ † ♥ † ♥ † ♥ † ♥ † ♥ † ♥ † ♥ † ♥ † ♥ † ♥ † ♥ † ♥ † ♥ † ♥ †

Thank you Lord
for giving my
dad back) temper
and all.

Grace

"Thank you Lord for giving my dad back, temper and all."

You wonder how this dad expressed his temper. Was he a spouse abuser? A child abuser? Or was he just a hothead—a verbal abuser? Perhaps he was all three.

Regardless, his offspring was ready and grateful to get him back, temper and all. Theologians have a name for this kind of acceptance. They call it grace—giving people what they need, not just what they have earned.

Forrest Gump, growing up in a broken home with a deformity of the spinal column, stood in need of grace.

The physician informed his mother that her only son's back was shaped like a question mark, "crooked as a politician." Part of Forrest's therapy was to wear clunky, unsightly braces on both legs. On the first day of school, after his mom put him on the bus, not one kid scooted over to make room for the disabled boy—until he got almost to the back of the bus. There Jenny broke the silence: "You can sit here if you want to." Grace. Pure gift.

Bob was born with multiple mental and physical handicaps. At fourteen, he could not read or write. He often stumbled and fell when he walked. One day, as he and his dad were taking a walk in a city park, they passed a baseball diamond where two teams of uniformed teenagers were playing. Bob's dad walked over to the coach and asked, "My son has never played baseball. Could he take a swing?" The coach laughed and said, "Hey, we're so many runs behind it won't make any difference—sure." Finally, in the last of the ninth inning, with the team only three runs behind, Bob was sent to the plate. The first pitch was a perfect strike, right down the middle. Bob just stood there, not knowing what to do. The pitcher, suddenly aware of Bob's disability, softly lobbed the second pitch underhanded, right over the plate. Bob didn't move. Strike two. Then one of the players leaped from the bench, jogged over to Bob, and said, "Here, let me help you."

Four hands on the bat, together they barely tapped the next pitch. It rolled several feet toward the pitcher. Bob and his new buddy ran together like crazy toward first. The catcher picked up the ball and deliberately threw it over the first baseman into right field. The right fielder retrieved the ball and flung it into left field. As Bob and his buddy were heading into third, the left fielder threw the ball into the bleachers behind third base. Bob and his buddy stomped on home plate together. Eighteen cheering, applauding baseball players and their coaches converged at home plate and mobbed Bob. There were high-fives and congratulatory hugs. The team hoisted Bob onto their shoulders. Bob laughed and cried. His new friends laughed and cried.

Grace happens. It happens whenever we give people what they need, not just what they have earned.

Give my Pappy the
wheel Power to
make
Surgery. threw his
EW his

Will

"Give my Pappy the wheelpower to make threw his surgery."

There is an invisible healing force, Norman Cousins wrote, that "can't be diagrammed or dissected; it can't be seen by topographic scanners and it can't be represented by the numbers on a medical chart. Yet it is the single most identifiable feature of human uniqueness. Unless it is understood and respected, all the other facts are secondary." Of this powerful force Shakespeare wrote, "Our bodies are our gardens, to which our wills are gardeners." Cousins and Shakespeare refer to what the child in the chapel termed "wheelpower"—the will (the wheels) to live.

Walter Cannon, a physiology professor at Harvard Medical School, conducted the twentieth century's definitive study of voodoo. He examined many cases from around the world of perfectly healthy physical specimens who were hexed by a witch doctor and died within days or even hours. His investigation, which included autopsies and interviews with many eyewitnesses, found that the cause of death was not poison. It was not trauma. Cannon concluded that the voodoo victim died from "a fatal power of the imagination." The cursed man, in his own mind, accepted an appointment with death. His tribe, wanting nothing to do with a cursed man, withdrew, leaving him feeling totally isolated—excommunicated, a man without a country. His "fatal power of the imagination"—believing that he was lost and undone and that there was nothing he could do to change his fate—translated into the cells and tissues of his body. It lowered his blood pressure and cut off oxygen to his vital organs and struck him dead. Losing the will to live, Cannon concluded from his study of voodoo, is lethal.

What is the place of "wheelpower" in the growing child? Just mentioning the subject, for the most part, strikes fear in the heart of parents. How many books and magazine articles have been published in our time on how to rear "the strong-willed child"? The most common word associations are rebellious, defiant, outspoken, stubborn, and irrepressible. Clashes of will between parent and child are frustrating and exhausting. But the child's indomitable will, *well channeled,* is one of life's greatest gifts. Strong-willed children become "movers and shakers"—adults who change the world. They meet challenges as if it is impossible for them to fail. And should it ever come to a hospitalization, no personal quality is more predictive of a good outcome than a strong will.

We hope early on to program into our kids' hard drives the sentence, "I think I can." Before they can read, we read them the story of *The Little Engine That Could.* We praise the determination and persistence of the little blue engine that tugged and pulled, pulled and tugged, puffed and chugged to get over the mountain and deliver toys to the children.

We know from experience that they're going to need "I think I can" in their repertoire. They'll be calling on wheelpower throughout life if they are going to be able to scale life's mountains and deliver the goods.

✝♥✝♥✝♥✝♥✝♥✝♥✝♥✝♥✝♥✝♥✝♥✝♥✝♥✝♥✝♥✝♥✝

Please pray for my
unborn baby for I am
only fourteen years old.

✝♥✝♥✝♥✝♥✝♥✝♥✝♥✝♥✝♥✝♥✝♥✝♥✝♥✝♥✝♥✝♥✝

What Child Is This?

"Please pray for my unborn baby for I am only four-teen years old."

What *mother* is this? Did she mean to get pregnant? Did her birth control fail her? Does she know who the father is? Was she raped? Do her parents know? Does she feel shame? Will she try to hide the pregnancy? Will she get prenatal care? Will she take good care of her health? Will she keep the baby? Will she stay in school? Will she graduate? Will she marry?

What *father* is this? Does he know about the pregnancy? Does he care about the mother? Does he want a baby? Will he push for an abortion? Will he be present at the delivery? Is he older than the mother? Does he have other babies? Does he want the baby to have his name? Will he get involved in rearing the child? Does he have a job? Will he pay child support?

What *child* is this? Will she, or he, be born premature? Have birth defects? Grow up in poverty? Have siblings? Be loved? Is this child, as Dylan Thomas described himself, "double-crossed" from his mother's womb?

Odds and averages, statistics and trends, fortunately, will not determine this child's fate. As Jesse Jackson said before the 1988 Democratic National Convention, "I was born in a slum, but the slum was not born in me. And it wasn't born in you. You can make it."

Booker T. Washington was born into slavery. After becoming one of the great scientists of his day he wrote, "I have been a slave once in my life—a slave in body. But I have since resolved that no inducement and no influence would ever make me a slave in soul, in my love for humanity, and in my search for truth."

Epictetus grew up a crippled slave, but he became a great Stoic philosopher and author. In his *Discourses* he wrote: "I must die, but must I die groaning? I must be imprisoned, but must I whine as well? I must suffer exile, but can anything prevent me from going in grace and with peace? Chain me? My leg you can chain, but my will, no."

Carol Burnett's parents were both alcoholics. Charlie Chaplin, who grew up in a London slum, at age five saw his father die and his mother go insane. Rod McKuen ran away from home at age eleven because his stepfather beat him, breaking his arm and ribs.

History's preeminent figure was born to a peasant girl who was not married. Scholars think that Mary was most likely a young teenager. Who would have bet one thin drachma that this baby, beginning life so humbly, might ever amount to much?

This teenager in the chapel, this child-having-a-child, perhaps felt unworthy to pray. She entered the chapel to ask others to pray—not for herself—but for her unborn baby. Who really knows what this child, "double-crossed" from the mother's womb, will be?

All things are possible.

God help

You Are My Sunshine

"God help"

Suppose you were six years old. And suppose you wanted to draw a picture of a giant, benevolent spirit. What image would most likely spring to mind?

Old Sol is the hands-down choice. Sunshine means children can go out to play. Sunshine conjures up pleasant memories (or fantasies) of vacations at the beach, ball games, field trips to the zoo or the park.

Ancient peoples worshiped the sun. Their life and well-being depended on the sun. Sunshine made their corn grow and berries ripen. It helped heat their dwellings. Small wonder that they began to call the first day of each week *Sun*day.

Old Sol trumps the darkness and symbolizes hope. "Dawn" consistently makes the top ten lists of the most beautiful sounds in the English language. The first stirrings of dawn bring an end to the longest or the scariest night. Dawn means hope. So Little Orphan Annie bellows at the top of her lungs that the sun will come out tomorrow.

But the sun has a shadow side. Sunshine makes human skin blister and burn. Sun parches crops, brings drought and famine. So theologians struggle with the ultimate question: "Does God, like the sun, have a shadow side? Can human suffering somehow fit within God's stupendous power?"

Goethe on his deathbed reportedly exclaimed, "More light!" Unamuno, the Spanish philosopher and writer, critiqued Goethe's dying words. He said that Goethe should have prayed for more warmth, because "we are dying of cold and not of darkness. It is not the night that kills, but the frost." Maybe Goethe and Unamuno are both right. Our souls crave light (enlightenment, insight, wisdom) and warmth (relationships, bonds, love) as well.

†♥†♥†♥†♥†♥†♥†♥†♥†♥†♥†♥†♥†♥†♥†♥†♥†♥†

God I hope I'll feel
better soon because
my birthday is coming
up and I dont want
to be in the hospital
at that time. So I want
to get real better for
my family and my animals
and friends. And I miss
everyone I know.

†♥†♥†♥†♥†♥†♥†♥†♥†♥†♥†♥†♥†♥†♥†♥†♥†♥†

Once I was called to be with the family of a patient who had died. Gathered around the bed were six or seven grandchildren. I suggested that we form a circle around the bed and hold hands and offer a prayer of thanksgiving for the grandfather's life. A split second before I began the prayer, one of the grandchildren began to sing softly, "You are my sunshine . . ." We all joined in the singing. And the crying. We lifted up "You Are My Sunshine" as our prayer of thanksgiving.

The six-year-old in the chapel is a good theologian! He believes that God is good, shedding light and warmth, like the sun.

Bellybuttons

"God I hope I'll feel better soon because my birthday is coming up and I don't want to be in the hospital at that time. So I want to get real better for my family and my animals and friends. And I miss everyone I know."

Did Adam have a navel? Regardless of what you think about Adam, our bodies all carry a sign that once we were not alone. Our navels remind us of the utopia from which we come, the genuinely good old days in the womb when life was comfortable and secure, when we were at one with another. All of our stories, in a very real sense, are stories of how successfully we transition out of and away from that cocoon and form satisfying new attachments.

In the first months and years of life, a pacifier helps us with that transition. We call the pacifier a "fooler"— it fools us into thinking our lips are attaching to mother's nipple. Little ones carry their favorite blanket with them whenever they leave home because it stands for the original security they felt in mother's womb and arms. The child who goes to the hospital shouldn't leave home without his or her dolls. It is not at all unusual for a teenage boy to bring a fuzzy, cuddly stuffed animal or two with him to the hospital. Could it be that we humans are "wired" for companionship? Is there something primal, something in our basic nature that wants to hold and to be held, to be cuddled and to cuddle?

The ancient Greeks certainly thought so. According to their oldest mythology, the god Eros created the earth a harmonious whole. But then the god Chaos came along and split everything in two. Ever since, all creation has been trying to bridge that gap, overcome that separation, and get back to original oneness.

The ancient Hebrews certainly thought so. According to the Torah, after creating the first human being,

God said, "It is not good for the human being to be alone" (Gen. 2:18). Aloneness, according to Genesis, is not our original state. Or our destiny.

A children's hospital understands that hell, for the young child, is separation from parents. In the intensive-care unit, where parents may not be allowed to stay with their baby, staff do their best to compensate. Massage therapists rub and stroke the newborn's spine, arms and legs, fingers and toes. Studies show that these stroked babies gain weight faster and go home sooner. Volunteer "grandparents" hold, cuddle, rock, and sing to the neonate. Nurses wind and rewind the newborn's music box, play nursery rhymes on a tape recorder, and cheer the baby on: "Come on, Ashley, you can do it." With a pinch on the baby's cheek the nurse affectionately adds, "Have I told you lately that I love you?" The child's humanity—that part of his or her being that thrives on touch and tenderness—must be saved.

Humans are not designed for aloneness. May we all live connected all the days of our life.

✝♥✝♥✝♥✝♥✝♥✝♥✝♥✝♥✝♥✝♥✝♥✝♥✝♥✝♥✝♥✝♥✝

help my mom to eat better
and make her use the
phone card wisely.
A. M. E. N.

✝♥✝♥✝♥✝♥✝♥✝♥✝♥✝♥✝♥✝♥✝♥✝♥✝♥✝♥✝♥✝♥✝

Copycats

"Help my mom to eat better and make her use the phone card wisely. A.M.E.N."

Children live what they learn. Walt Whitman, in *Autumn Rivulets*, offers the classic statement of this fact.

There was a child went forth every day,
And the first object he look'd upon
That object he became,
And that object became part of him
For the day or a certain part of the day
Or for many years
Or stretching cycles of years.

Whitman proceeds to detail the many persons, places, and things that leave their mark on the developing child, from the morning glories to the village drunkard to the dining-room furniture. We all are, like Tennyson's Ulysses, a part of all that we have met. Is there any doubt that the child in the chapel, praying for Mother to use the phone card wisely, is repeating words from the mouth of an adult, most likely Father?

What is the place of parents in child-rearing? Their place is gigantic—but it is not absolute. Some seem to think that rearing a child is like baking a cake. You get a tried and true recipe, add a pinch of this and a dash of that, and presto—one day out comes the cake of your dreams. This cookbook approach is naïve because too many dynamics lie outside the parents' control. At conception, when the parents' sex cells unite, a new being with a unique constitution is on the way. The child's unique temperament may lack "goodness of fit" with the personalities of the parents. A frisky child, for example, may be born to laid-back parents, or vice versa. The child's unique temperament is going to find expression, despite the best and worst that parents do. The cookbook approach to child-rearing also discounts the power of peer pressures and cultural influences that become huge in the teenage years. It also discounts the built-in developmental need and freedom each child has to individuate, to become different from parents, to find one's own way in the world.

The child who wrote the prayer for Mom to use the phone card more wisely was parroting someone else's words. She, or a sibling in the same house, might have perceived and interpreted the situation differently. She might have prayed for Dad to be more understanding of Mom's need to talk to family and friends. Or for Dad to improve his communication skills with Mom. Or for Dad to have more of a social life himself. Each child chooses to conform to or rebel against parents' interpretations of things. Most will do a little of both.

Recognizing parents' limited powers in child-rearing led Francis Bacon to call parents and children "hostages to fortune." Whether we interpret it as blind chance, God's will, astrological influence, or karmic overflow from a previous existence, "fortune" stands for all the aspects of what a child becomes that lie outside the parents' control.

Our aim is to be responsible *to* our children, knowing we cannot ultimately be responsible *for* who they are and what they become.

✝♥✝♥✝♥✝♥✝♥✝♥✝♥✝♥✝♥✝♥✝♥✝♥✝♥✝♥✝♥✝♥✝

Please help me
make it through
the night without
Saying something
wrong to Dr. L.

✝♥✝♥✝♥✝♥✝♥✝♥✝♥✝♥✝♥✝♥✝♥✝♥✝♥✝♥✝♥✝♥✝

Night

"Please help me make it through the night without saying something wrong to Dr. L."

Night has its terrors. Creaks in the floor. Real or imaginary figures moving about. Bad dreams. Wind sounds.

Ancient peoples thought the howling night winds came from demons and devils out in the desert. To ward off the evil spirits, our Cornish ancestors prayed, "From ghoulies and ghosties and long-leggedty beasties and things that go bump in the night, Good Lord, deliver us."

For many of us, the first prayer we memorized and

said before going to bed addressed the dangers of the night: "Now I lay me down to sleep. I pray the Lord my soul to keep. If I should die before I wake, I pray the Lord my soul to take." Night has its terrors. A child can lose a soul, or a life, in the night.

Parents who sit up all night with a sick child keenly sense the terrible possibilities of the night. Legions of us, longing for dawn's early light, have prayed, "Just let us make it through this one night." According to the Torah, the tenth and most devastating plague—the killing of the firstborn in every Egyptian family—came at the stroke of midnight. Elie Wiesel titled his Pulitzer Prize–winning chronicle of the evils of the Holocaust, which included the execution of children, *Night*. For conscientious parents, night stands for the host of threatening "principalities and powers" outside our control.

Night in a strange place, with strange people, has terrors all its own for the hospitalized child. For some, it is their first night away from home. And, if the child is in an intensive-care unit, the child and parents may be separated all night. But thanks to wonderfully nurturing nurses, the separation usually troubles the parents more than the child.

An equally daunting challenge for the hospitalized child is figuring out how to relate to the bigger-than-life, god-like physician. I visited a teenage boy one morning who had fretted all night over what his physician said. He had heard his physician say the day before, "We're between a rocket and a hearse." For twenty-four hours the boy pondered the meaning of those ominous words. I called the physician, who told me his actual words had been, "We're between a rock and a hard place." Those words would not have troubled the teenager, because he knew he was between a rock and a hard place. But there was no rocket, much less a hearse, in sight. The teenager and his parents had been too intimidated by the physician to ask him what he meant.

How can God help the child, little or grown, who prays for help to make it through the night? Through prayer, we trust the child will come to know the same solace that prompted the Psalmist to write, "You will not fear the terror of the night, nor the pestilence that stalks in darkness. God will deliver you from the snare of the fowler and from the deadly pestilence; God will cover you with his pinions, and under his wings you will find refuge" (Ps. 91).

✝♥✝

Dear God,
I'm 10 yrs old and I'm in the hospital! I hope to go home soon, Sunday. Please make my leg better so I can walk. The man that hit me   please forgive him. He probably didn't know what he was doing. I love you God very much.   Amen

✝♥✝

A Hard Law

"Dear God, I'm 10 yrs. old. . . . Please make my leg better so I can walk. The man that hit me please forgive him. He probably didn't know what he was doing. . . ."

How did this little girl come by her alternative values? Someone at home or church had to have taught her to imitate one who prayed for those who were killing him, "Forgive them, because they don't know what they are doing" (Luke 23:34).

At ten years of age, she is taking a road less traveled. Not the one traveled by Captain Ahab, obsessed with vengeance against the great white whale who had amputated his leg. Captain Ahab lived by the conventional wisdom that "revenge is sweet." Not the one traveled by the movie and television action heroes. They become heroes by way of "one up-ing" their adversaries. They live by the conventional wisdom, "Don't get mad, get even." Not traveled by parents who aim to raise their kids "value free," who just want their kids to "do their own thing," to do what comes naturally. That conventional wisdom is articulated by Shakespeare's Shylock: "If you prick us, do we not bleed? If you tickle us, do we not laugh? If you poison us, do we not die? And if you wrong us, shall we not revenge?"

Mahatma Gandhi, using the principle of passive resistance, succeeded in freeing India from British rule. To those who criticized Gandhi for not taking a more militant approach, he explained, "An eye for an eye and a tooth for a tooth just leaves a lot of people blind and toothless."

One of America's great advice columnists, Abigail Van Buren, offered her wisdom to those who sought help in dealing with enemies: "People who fight fire with fire usually end up with ashes."

A handsome, affluent lawyer, William Stanton, came up against Abraham Lincoln in an 1854 court case. One of his tactics was to mock Lincoln's physical appearance. He said that Lincoln "belonged to the apes." He repeatedly referred to Lincoln as "the gawky, long-armed ape." When Lincoln became president, he appointed Stanton his Secretary of War.

In *Too Late the Phalarope*, Alan Paton, who made many enemies in his efforts to bring an end to apartheid in South Africa, writes of revenge, bitterness, and rejection. The story centers on a father, Jacob, who could never bring himself to forgive his son Pieter for a crime Pieter had committed as a young man. There was, however, one potentially redemptive moment late in their relationship. On Jacob's birthday, Pieter gave his dad a book about birds. For one brief shining moment, the two enjoyed a discussion of the phalarope, a South African bird. But it was too little too late. That one conversation, sweet as it was, could not alone atone for decades of hostility. The phalarope had come too late. Of forgiveness delayed, Paton writes, "There's a hard law that when a deep injury is done to us, we never recover until we forgive."

The ten-year-old in the chapel is on the road to recovery, body and soul. It's a hard law.

✝♥✝♥✝♥✝♥✝♥✝♥✝♥✝♥✝♥✝♥✝♥✝♥✝♥✝♥✝♥✝♥✝♥✝♥✝♥✝

Dear Lord,
Please help mime
and papaw not
be SCARED,
A little GIRL
WRote this

✝♥✝♥✝♥✝♥✝♥✝♥✝♥✝♥✝♥✝♥✝♥✝♥✝♥✝♥✝♥✝♥✝♥✝♥✝♥✝

Little Girls

"Dear Lord, Please help mime and papaw not be scared. A little girl wrote this."

Dear little girl,

Thank you for sharing your concern for your mime and papaw. You are very fortunate to have good grandparents. Many little girls do not. I know it hurts you to see them scared. We will hope and pray with you that God will give them courage while they are in the hospital.

You are a very special little girl. I like the way you expressed your feelings on the prayer card. Some children are too timid to do that. I can tell that you love your grandparents very much. Those two qualities—boldness and loving kindness—will serve you well in life, both now as a little girl, and later when you are a grown woman.

Many of the fairy-tale stories little girls grow up hearing, like Cinderella or Snow White, suggest that, for females to do well, they must be beautiful and must be rescued by a male. That is not true of all fairy tales. Do you know the story of Hansel and Gretel? When they were abandoned in the Black Forest by their stepmother, a witch caged Hansel to fatten him and eat him. It was Gretel, the little girl, who pushed the witch inside the oven and slammed the door and freed her brother. Because of Gretel's boldness in the face of great danger, and her loving kindness for her brother and father, the little girl is the hero in this story.

The movie *Ever After* retells the story of Cinderella. When, just like in the Cinderella story, Danielle's father suddenly dies and she is left in the care of a mean stepmother, the little girl uses her wits *and* her sweetness, her pride *and* her basic goodness, to overcome problems. When she gets older and her prince comes calling, Danielle refuses to submit graciously to his leadership. Instead, she insists that the prince respect her and treat her as his equal. I hope you will be like Danielle—strong *and* kind, spirited *and* loving, intelligent *and* attractive. Like Danielle, you need all of these if you are going to be successful handling the many difficulties and pains of growing up.

Anne Frank is a good example for little girls like you. Anne kept a diary, which might be a good idea for you, too. As a young teenager, she witnessed many of her neighbors and friends being taken away and murdered by evil people. She ended up being murdered too, but not before she wrote in her diary, "I've found that there is always some beauty in life—in nature, sunshine, freedom, in yourself; these can all help you. Look at these things, then you find yourself again, and God, and then you regain your balance."

You may be a little girl, but you already have balance. Balance will help you deal with whatever comes, including the health problems your grandparents have. Be sweet. And be bold. And God will provide you with as much love and courage as you need.

Sincerely,
The hospital chaplain

✝♥✝♥✝♥✝♥✝♥✝♥✝♥✝♥✝♥✝♥✝♥✝♥✝♥✝♥✝♥✝♥✝♥✝

Please help my grand
Get out of the hospital!!!!
and PleAse help him get
Well and out!!!!!!

✝♥✝♥✝♥✝♥✝♥✝♥✝♥✝♥✝♥✝♥✝♥✝♥✝♥✝♥✝♥✝♥✝♥✝

! ! ! ! !

"Please help my grandpa!!!! Get out of the hospital!!!! And please help him get well and out!!!!!!"

The child empties his hot heart. There is no contentment in his soul. No ambiguity. No religiously correct formulations coming forth. With no English teacher around to correct his punctuation, the child protests, pounding on heaven's door: "Get my grandpa out of here!!!"

Contrast his passion with the touchstone of our time—"comfort." We crave comfortable lifestyles. We manage our finances so we can be comfortable in our old age. Never wanting to offend, we sophisticated adults say, politely, "I'm comfortable with this. How about you?" We prefer peace over striving, placidity over activism, equanimity over passion. We seek a life with more light and less heat.

Voices from the past call into question our comfort icon. Thomas Jefferson wrote, "Something pursued with ardor is necessary to guard us from *tedium vitae* (the tedium of life)." Albert Einstein said, "I have never looked on ease and happiness as ends in themselves—that's the ideal of a pigsty." The ancient Greeks over their gymnasiums sometimes inscribed this admonition: *"Strip and Run or Retire."* Scripture implores, "Whatever your hand finds to do, do it with all your might" (Eccl. 9:10).

Christy Brown, one of Ireland's most popular novelists, began life crippled with cerebral palsy. Christy had control over only one part of his body—his left foot. One of twenty-two children, at age five he was able to seize a piece of chalk from his sister's hand with his left foot. Grasping the chalk between his first and second left toe, he wrote the letter "A" on the floor, convincing his family that he was not retarded. At age ten, on Christmas morning he found himself "hot with excitement" over a box of paints and brushes that had been given to, but rejected by, one of his brothers. He taught himself to hold a brush in his left foot and paint. By age seventeen Christy Brown was typing stories with his left foot, producing stories that made him one of Ireland's most loved writers. Of his career as a writer and painter, Brown later wrote, "If I couldn't know the joy of dancing, I could still know the ecstasy of creating."

One hears echoes in this child's prayer of Emily Dickinson: "O Jesus! in the air, I know not which thy chamber is—I'm knocking everywhere."

Sometimes the fitting punctuation mark, in prayer life or in many other aspects of life, is not a question mark or a period or a comma. Sometimes what is most needed is to cut through all the clutter and punctuate life with a "hot with excitement" exclamation point!

✝♥✝

Lord,
    Why didn't you answer
my prayers? My pappy's
dieing and my family
has already been through
enough. Please help us to be
strong, Lord.

✝♥✝

Why, God?

"Lord, Why didn't you answer my prayers? My pappy's dieing and my family has already been through enough."

All of us, like this child, sooner or later confront the why-do-good-people-suffer tar baby. Our boxing match with the tar baby takes place on two levels. On the emotional level, "why" is a cry of protest and outrage at the injustice of life. A good listener or counselor understands the pain prompting the questions, acknowledges it, and commiserates: "I don't understand either. Makes me angry too. Sure does seem unfair." For young children, a knowing, reassuring hug or embrace may be the most fitting response to their essentially visceral expression.

But as we grow, and develop cognitively, our inquiring minds want to know. Is there any sense to suffering? A hidden meaning? A purpose? A logical, cause-effect explanation? Or is it, as Shakespeare wrote, a meaningless "tale told by an idiot, full of sound and fury, signifying nothing"?

Here are our best attempts at an answer:

1. There is a God who is in control, who has a plan for the universe, who knows best, and who either wills or allows suffering to further God's grand plan. God will more than compensate all the suffering of this life in a hereafter. Some, however, chafe at this image of a god that resembles a cosmic abusive parent, who tortures children or allows them to be tortured with an "I know what's best for you" or "this is for your own good" rationale.

2. There is a devil, a Satan, who is responsible for all evil and suffering, not God, who is only good. But some resist the idea of a god who cannot or will not leash or "take out" the tormentor of innocent children.

3. The universe runs on natural law. There is a scientific cause for everything. Don't look for hidden

meanings. What you see is what you get—period. Some, however, as Engelhardt said, ". . . reel at the thought that all may exist, that the entire universe may exist, for no reason."

4. A recycling process is at work in the universe, promoting those who suffer in this incarnation to something higher next time. Just as the seasons continue to change, so we disappear and reappear again and again, evolving or devolving each time according to how we live. This is Eastern philosophy, probably held by more humans than any other view. Some argue that there is absolutely no evidence that this process metes out justice.

5. God is absolute love, symbolized by the cross of Christ. God comes to us in our suffering, supporting us with strength and courage and limitless love. But this God is still in process, evolving, limited in power, not tightly in control of nature. Some say this God—watching and caring from the sidelines but unable to intervene and change things—is more to be pitied than worshiped.

All our seeking may ultimately end, as it began, in humility before the great mystery called life. And in respect for fellow-seekers who understand it differently.

✝♥✝♥✝♥✝♥✝♥✝♥✝♥✝♥✝♥✝♥✝♥✝♥✝♥✝♥✝♥✝♥✝

Thank you God
for large and
small miracles.

✝♥✝♥✝♥✝♥✝♥✝♥✝♥✝♥✝♥✝♥✝♥✝♥✝♥✝♥✝♥✝♥✝

Miracles

"Thank you God for large and small miracles."

Do miracles really happen? Does God ever interrupt the natural order of things? Did God perform miracles once upon a time, but no more? Should belief in miracles be relegated to a pre-scientific, rife-with-superstition world? Does belief in miracles require us to suspend our rationality and believe in magic?

Albert Einstein, hardly a Neanderthal, wrote, "There are only two ways to live your life. One is as though nothing is a miracle. The other is as though everything is. I choose to think it is the latter."

That we *are*—that there is something instead of

nothing—surely is the biggest miracle of all. Oxford mathematician Sir Roger Penrose calculates how unlikely, how improbable, how almost infinitely impossible it would be for advanced life-forms on the earth to have happened as the result of blind chance. The odds—one in ten to the 123rd power. That number, he explains, is too big to be written down in full even if every proton in the entire universe had one digit written on it.

Some scientists take a macro-view of the universe and see miracle; some take a micro-view and see miracle. Nineteenth-century physiologist Johann Caspar Lavater, awed by detail he observed under the microscope, exclaimed, "Each particle of matter is an immensity; each leaf a world; each insect an inexplicable compendium."

Some, like Spanish cellist Pablo Casals, see miracle in a child: "Do you know what you are? You are a marvel. You are unique. In all the world there is no other child exactly like you. In the millions of years that have passed there has never been another child like you. And look at your body. What a wonder it is! Your legs, your arms, your cunning fingers, the way you move! You may become a Shakespeare, a Michelangelo, a

Beethoven. You have the capacity for anything. Yes, you are a marvel."

Some of us see miracle regularly in a children's hospital. A pediatric oncologist, asked by a reporter how his staff copes with caring for children who have cancer, answered, "We expect at least one miracle every day."

What is a miracle? A miracle is a wonder-full, often unexpected, often unlikely, often inexplicable turn of events. Which is a "large" and which is a "small" miracle? Is a child cured of cancer by chemotherapy and radiation more or less a miracle than the child whose tumor "spontaneously" disappears? Is the one-pound neonate saved by a ventilator and other life-support systems any more or less a miracle than the birth of a healthy baby?

Miracles? Those who have a child's eyes to see, Einstein might say, will see.

†♥†♥†♥†♥†♥†♥†♥†♥†♥†♥†♥†♥†♥†♥†♥†♥†♥†♥†♥†

Dear GOd,
I have a Sick
Sister I WISH
you woo dHave
a potion For
her. llovehel Better
tHAN iNe thiNG
iN the woNLd

†♥†♥†♥†♥†♥†♥†♥†♥†♥†♥†♥†♥†♥†♥†♥†♥†♥†♥†♥†

Magic Potion

"Dear God, I have a sick sister I wish you wood have a potion for her. I love her better than inething in the world."

Hospitals stand as citadels of hope in our society. We expect that once we call 911, once the ambulance arrives, once we make it to a hospital emergency room, once the right medicine or surgery is adminis-tered—everything will, with tincture of time, end well. In an era when we have mapped the human genome, surely a solution can be found somewhere out there for whatever ails us.

Just please make it sooner than later! In our

fast-food, drive-through-flu-shot society, we expect the pharmacy to produce a magic pill the way Harry Potter conjures up a magic potion. We expect instant results. And if the pharmacy doesn't stock it, it can probably be found and flown in from afar in only a matter of hours.

Unfortunately, for many sick or injured, no magic potion exists. The elevator to wellness is broken, and they have to take the stairs. Wilma Rudolph, one of twenty-two brothers and sisters growing up in Bethlehem, Tennessee, began life sick. She was stricken with polio, scarlet fever, and double pneumonia. She had to wear a leg brace from age six to eleven. But her mother, brothers, and sisters gave her physical therapy four times a day for years. Wilma eventually set the world record for the two-hundred-meter run and won three gold medals at the 1960 Rome Olympics. The little crippled girl became the fastest woman runner in the world. With no magic potion available, persistence and tender loving care from family and friends brought healing. Healing is often like that—painfully slow. It takes weeks, months, years. Healing has to take the stairs.

This is most true of wounds to the spirit. These invisible wounds heal painfully slowly. A coronary artery bypass surgery heals in weeks. But a heart with a hole left in it by a child's death takes months and years, even a lifetime. On the same day that a fourteen-year-old boy killed three classmates in a high school lobby in West Paducah, Kentucky, area ministers and counselors called for the healing to begin. On the next day they were speaking of the need for closure.

But closing wounds prematurely can be dangerous and even work against healing. The wounds that heal best are those that heal from the inside out. When skin is closed over a wound too quickly, the tissue festers. Toxins get trapped inside and can't get out. In time, dark pus oozes forth. If it doesn't burst on its own, the wound has to be reopened and irrigated. A new fistula (passage) has to be created to release the poisons.

We hope, like the child, that a magic potion is available somewhere. But if the elevator to health is broken, we have to take the stairs. And lean on friends to steady us. And catch us should we fall.

✝♥✝♥✝♥✝♥✝♥✝♥✝♥✝♥✝♥✝♥✝♥✝♥✝♥✝♥✝♥✝♥✝♥✝

13 years old 9 months   6 days
1:35 P.M.
I think my spleen is enlarged

I hope I live to be very old!

If I don't, Lord, please take
care of my mother! Help my
Father who has hurt me. but
I have forgiven him! Help him
to be a good husband and to be
O.K. through all that happens!

Lord, have mercy on me

✝♥✝♥✝♥✝♥✝♥✝♥✝♥✝♥✝♥✝♥✝♥✝♥✝♥✝♥✝♥✝♥✝♥✝

Forgive Everyone Everything!

"I think my spleen is enlarged. I hope I live to be very old! If I don't, Lord, please take care of my mother! Help my father who has hurt me. But I have forgiven him!"

I knew this patient. I admired and loved her very much. When she wrote this prayer, she was "13 years old, 9 months 6 days" old. She suffered all of her life with a chronic condition, and she knew at the time she wrote the prayer that her departure time was near. In the intensive-care unit, on a ventilator and with a tube down her throat, she could not talk. But she could write.

I invited her to write out her prayer on a legal pad and let me leave it in the chapel for others to read. She died three days later. This is Sarah's prayer.

"I think my spleen is enlarged." Hospital patients crave information and whatever experts interpret the data to mean. Sometimes dwelling on details (the trees) is easier for all involved than to consider the big picture (the woods). It is far less threatening for the physician and the family and the teenage patient to talk about an enlarged spleen than it is to talk about imminent death.

"I hope I live to be very old." Denial is one of God's most merciful gifts. Denial buffers and shields us from the threat of nonexistence. Who would dare take a gram of hope away from a thirteen-year-old whose entire being screams "I want to live!"?

"Lord, please take care of my mother." I have been with thousands of people as they lay dying. Their foremost concern—children and adults alike—is rarely fear of hell or hope of heaven. It is almost always the ultimate angst of separation from, and concern for, their nearest and dearest. This was true of Jesus, who, just before breathing his last, made provision for his mother's welfare.

"Help my father who has hurt me. But I have forgiven him." Sports columnist Mitch Albom learned the importance of forgiveness from Morrie Schwartz, one of his favorite college professors at Brandeis University. Twenty years after college, Albom learned that Professor Schwartz was dying of Lou Gehrig's disease. He arranged to visit the dying professor for fourteen Tuesdays in 1995, sitting at his feet and gleaning insights about the meaning of life, the kind of insights that often only the dying can have. Out of those conversations came the best-selling book, *Tuesdays With Morrie*. Morrie's final wisdom from his deathbed on how to live robustly: "Forgive everyone everything!"

Take it from an old man who is dying. Or from a teenage girl who is dying. Their message, as they leave this world for the next, is consistent, and it is wise: *Forgive everyone everything*—even a family member who has deeply hurt you.

✝♥✝♥✝♥✝♥✝♥✝♥✝♥✝♥✝♥✝♥✝♥✝♥✝♥✝♥✝♥✝

hello! My name
is Holly. And I
feel Sorry for
these people

✝♥✝♥✝♥✝♥✝♥✝♥✝♥✝♥✝♥✝♥✝♥✝♥✝♥✝♥✝♥✝

Feelings

"Hello! My name is Holly. And I feel sorry for these people."

Visitors to the hospital chapel sometimes read prayers left on the altar and feel moved to act. One person returned with a grocery bag full of snacks and pinned a note to it: "Please take and eat while you wait." One returned with two shopping bags full of toys. One returned with a box of one hundred Ziggy dolls and a note of instruction to give the dolls to sick children. All three gifts were anonymous gifts, gifts straight from the heart.

Psychiatrist Willard Gaylin gave his book *Feelings*

the subtitle *Our Vital Signs*. Our capacity to feel for others distinguishes us from rocks and brutes, Rambos and robots, oysters and carrots and sociopathic personalities. Our vital signs—signs that our humanity is alive and well—are the feelings for others that find expression.

Norman Cousins, in a *Saturday Review* editorial many years ago, claimed that the highest expression of any civilization is not to be found in its literature, its art, its music, its educational system, its military strength, its abundance, or its religiosity. A civilization's highest expression is the tenderness its members feel for one another. If America is breaking down, Cousins insisted, it is not because we lack the brains to fix things. It is because our feelings are being dulled.

Anthropologist Margaret Mead was asked by a student for the earliest sign of civilization in a society. Is it a clay pot? A fishhook? A stone for grinding grain? A drawing on a rock? Her answer: a healed femur. No healed femurs, she explained, are found among savages. Skulls crushed by clubs, yes. Temples pierced by arrows, yes. But no healed femurs. A healed femur means that someone showed compassion. Someone had to care for the person with the broken leg while it healed. Someone had to do the hunting and bring in the food while the injured person was disabled. No healed femurs are found where a survival-of-the-fittest, law-of-the-jungle mentality reigns. Compassion, according to Mead, is the first indication of being civilized.

In the embryonic stage of human development, we grow our heart before we grow our skeleton. A heart can grow without a skeleton; a skeleton cannot grow without a heart. Many of us, postpartum, get those priorities reversed. We grow appearance first and soul second. Our frames look good; our inner selves need work.

Sometimes we come full circle, having learned from experience that materialism intimidates. Narcissism alienates. Hedonism manipulates. And provincialism isolates. But compassion—having a heart—opens us to one another. And grows civility. And makes civilization possible.

✝♥✝♥✝♥✝♥✝♥✝♥✝♥✝♥✝♥✝♥✝♥✝♥✝♥✝♥✝♥✝♥✝

✝♥✝♥✝♥✝♥✝♥✝♥✝♥✝♥✝♥✝♥✝♥✝♥✝♥✝♥✝♥✝♥✝

A Sacred Yes!

Adults, Art Linkletter said, are just kids who have lost their way.

Consider the old cowpoke who strolled into the hotel lobby. Disappointed to find the desk unattended, he pounded on the bell. The clerk, who had been stoking the fire in the dining room, finally appeared. The grizzled old cowpoke, tired and cross from a hard day on the trail, lit into him: "Your service here really stinks!" The clerk apologized profusely and gave him the key to the finest room in the house.

Now the clerk had a mischievous streak in him. Sometime past midnight, he sneaked into the snoring old cowpoke's room. He rubbed limburger cheese on his mustache and sneaked out.

The next morning, when the old cowpoke awoke and sat up in bed and began to wipe the sleep from his eyes, he smelled something awful. He got out of bed grimacing and sniffing around the room. He mumbled under his breath, "This room stinks!"

He threw his clothes on and beat a hasty charge to the lobby. There his nose picked up the familiar scent. "I came down here to complain that my room has an awful smell," he told the clerk who had given him the room, "but you know what—this whole hotel stinks."

He walked outside to get some fresh air, and the noxious smell followed him, strong as ever. He jumped on his horse and galloped away, protesting to bystanders on the wooden sidewalk, "Your town stinks!"

The last thing some observers near the outskirts of town heard him spit out, as he rode away furiously: "This whole #$%!&* world stinks!"

Children, by contrast, go out to greet life with a big "Yes!" emblazoned on their faces. That sparkle in their eyes originates in their souls, souls teeming with wonderment, amazement, and "look-out-world-here-I-come-ready-or-not" anticipation. Nietzsche marveled, "A child is innocent and forgetting, a new beginning, a game, a self-propelled wheel, a first movement, a sacred 'Yes!'" What a pity, as we grow up, to exchange that sacred Yes somewhere along the way for a piece of rotten-smelling cheese.

We don't know what health crisis brought the little girl to the hospital chapel. From her drawing, we know only that she brought with her two huge resources: (1) a sacred Yes, shining out of her soul onto her face, and (2) a heart of love, as big as her self.

And precisely here is the gospel, in all its simplicity, according to the children: (1) God gave you a mind—use it to say "Yes!" to life. (2) God gave you a big heart—use it to love others as you love yourself.

That's all that matters. World without end. Amen.